106

Greatest Piano Studies

ETUDES, DRILLS AND EXERCISES IN
PROGRESSIVE ORDER FOR THE
DEVELOPMENT OF TONE AND TECHNIC

COMPILED AND EDITED BY

HOWARD KASSCHAU

ED. 2429

G. SCHIRMER, Inc.

DISTRIBUTED BY

HAL•LEONARD®
CORPORATION
7777 W. BLUEMOUND RD. P.O. BOX 13819 MILWAUKEE, WI 53213

TO THE TEACHER

It is a necessary and rewarding responsibility to develop a growth in the technical ability of your student that parallels his growth in musicianship. Two elements contribute to a mastery of the keyboard:

Mastery of Tone, which requires the production of a succession of musical sounds that are firm and secure throughout the entire dynamic range from *pp* to *ff;*

Mastery of Technic, which requires the ability to deliver that succession of tones in varying speeds with complete accuracy and with a minimum of effort.

106 Greatest Piano Studies presents *in progressive order* those exercises, etudes, drills and studies that insure the successful development of Tone and Technic. These studies have been selected from the works of such master etude composers as Czerny, Burgmüller, Clementi, Bertini, Gurlitt and Heller as well as many others. They represent the finest studies for the development of various technical skills. All of the compositions in these volumes are presented in their original forms without simplification or abridgement. A minor exception has been made in studies 1 through 12. These studies have been lowered one octave to comply with modern pedagogy which teaches the Treble and Bass Clefs from the very beginning.

These volumes have been prepared to supply a maximum of interest and variety through the learning of the studies in consecutive order. Studies for the development of one particular technical skill have not been grouped together but have been interspersed among studies that develop other technical skills, thereby affording variety and interest. Metronome markings that are *realistic* in their representations of the speeds that your student should attain have been indicated for each study.

As new technics are introduced in progressive grade levels, earlier technics are further developed in expanded form, thereby insuring the well rounded technical growth of the student at all times. An outline in alphabetical order follows which affords a comprehensive picture in five grade levels of the material contained in these volumes and the purposes for which this material has been selected.

VOLUME I

Elementary

Studies for the development of finger action: Nos. 1 to 14.

Easy

Contrasting touch studies: Nos. 17, 19.
Five finger drills in extended positions: Nos. 15, 16, 24.
Interlaced passage studies: Nos. 25, 26, 27, 28.
Expression study: No. 18.
Pedal studies: Nos. 18, 22, 27.
Phrasing study: No. 29.
Rhythm study: No. 22.
Staccato study: No. 20.
Velocity study for both hands: No. 23.
Velocity study for the left hand: No. 30.
Velocity study for the right hand: No. 21.

Moderately Easy

Chord studies: Nos. 48, 49, 50, 53.
Contrasting touch studies: Nos. 40, 44, 47.
Cross hand studies: Nos. 42, 49.
Expression studies: Nos. 46, 50, 51.
Interlaced passage study: No. 49.
Pedal studies: Nos. 41, 42, 47, 49, 50.
Rhythm studies: Nos. 31, 45, 47.
Scale studies for both hands: Nos. 39, 41, 52.
Scale studies for the left hand: Nos. 55, 57.
Scale studies for the right hand: Nos. 54, 56.
Velocity studies for both hands: Nos. 43, 48.
Velocity studies for the left hand: Nos. 33, 35, 37.
Velocity studies for the right hand: Nos. 32, 34, 36, 38.

Slightly Advanced

Chord study: No. 59.
Expression studies: Nos. 59, 61, 62.
Velocity studies for both hands: Nos. 58, 60.

VOLUME II

Slightly Advanced

Arpeggio study: No. 65.
Chromatic scale study: No. 66.
Combined touch studies: Nos. 73, 80, 84.
Double note studies: Nos. 63, 69, 71, 85.
Expression studies: Nos. 67, 81, 86.
Pedal studies: Nos. 65, 67, 73, 81, 86.
Repeated note studies: Nos. 78, 79.
Scale studies: Nos. 66, 70.
Staccato study: No. 76.
Syncopation study: No. 77.
Velocity studies for both hands: Nos. 72, 80, 82, 83.
Velocity studies for the left hand: Nos. 64, 75.
Velocity studies for the right hand: Nos. 68, 74.

Moderately Difficult

Arpeggio study for both hands: No. 97.
Arpeggio study for the left hand: No. 99.
Arpeggio study for the right hand: No. 98.
Chord studies: Nos. 88, 105.
Combined touch study: No. 106.
Expression studies: Nos. 90, 91, 103, 105.
Interlaced passage studies: Nos. 92, 104.
Martellato study: No. 92.
Octave study: No. 101.
Pedal studies: Nos. 89, 90, 91, 96, 97, 103, 104, 105, 106.
Rubato study: No. 96.
Trill studies: Nos. 94, 95.
Turn study: No. 89.
Velocity studies: Nos. 87, 93, 100, 102.

106 Greatest Piano Studies has been compiled to supplement the Howard Kasschau Piano Course. They may be introduced on page 24 of *Teach Me To Play* and cover all technical requirements up to the middle of Book Four. However, these studies may be easily incorporated into any other organized system of piano instruction.

Howard Kasschau

The student should sit at the keyboard at such a height that the elbows are level with the top of the keys; the feet are placed together in front of the pedals. The elbows hang loosely at the sides and no tension should interfere with a free elbow movement. The forearm, wrist and hand form a level line; the fingers should be gently curved.

At the beginning the student should produce all tones with *finger action only*. He should be careful that the hand and forearm remain quiet. The basic touch is *legato*. All tones must be connected without a perceptible overlap of finger movement. This requires the release of a key at precisely the same instant that the next key is depressed.

Adolphe-Clair Le Carpentier
A Piano Method, First Exercise

Study for the development of independent finger action

Louis Köhler
Op. 218, No. 1

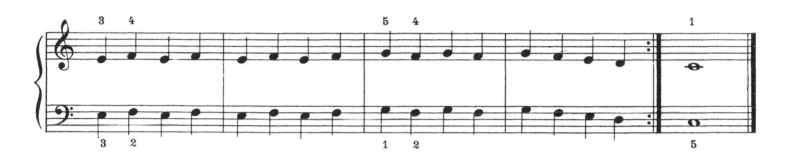

Study for the development of independent finger action

Louis Köhler
Op. 218, No. 2

In study No. 4 only the right hand contains the quarter-note rhythm of the preceding studies. Care must be taken that whole notes played by the left hand are connected from measure to measure. This must be done in the same manner as the right hand quarter-notes are connected from count to count.

Cornelius Gurlitt
Op. 82, No. 10

In study No. 5 only the left hand contains the quarter-note rhythm. Care must be taken that whole notes played by the right hand are connected from measure to measure. This must be done in the same manner as the left hand quarter-notes are connected from count to count.

Cornelius Gurlitt
Op. 82, No. 11

Study for the development of independent finger action

Louis Köhler
Op. 218, No. 3

In study No. 7 the notes of the right hand are imitated one measure later by the notes of the left hand. This style of composition is called a *canon*. It is important that the left hand be played with the same degrees of speed and loudness as the right hand. Only in this way can the effect of true imitation be produced.

Cornelius Gurlitt
Op. 82, No. 12

Study for the development of independent finger action

Adolphe-Clair Le Carpentier
A Piano Method, Second Exercise

Study for the development of independent finger action

Adolphe-Clair Le Carpentier
A Piano Method, Third Exercise

Study for the development of independent finger action

Adolphe-Clair Le Carpentier
A Piano Method, Fourth Exercise

Eighth-notes are introduced in the left hand part of study No.11. They must be played *legato*. It is important that the hand remain still and that the *legato* sound be produced by *finger action only*.

Conrad Kühner
School of Etudes, No.1

The eighth-note pattern of study No. 11 is reversed in study No. 12. Notice that in No. 11 the eighth-notes were employed in a $\frac{4}{4}$ rhythm; in study No.12 they are employed in a $\frac{3}{4}$ rhythm. The eighth-notes in the right hand part must be played *legato;* the *legato* sound should be produced by *finger action only*.

Conrad Kühner
School of Etudes, No.2

10

This kind of study is called a *five finger exercise*. It is designed for the practice of the co-ordination of both hands. Notice that the ascending notes of the pattern in the right hand are fingered 1 2 3 4 5 and the ascending notes of the pattern in the left hand are fingered 5 4 3 2 1. The fingerings of both hands are reversed as the notes descend. In a *five finger exercise* it is important that both hands play with equal strength and that all tones are evenly spaced.

Adolphe-Clair Le Carpentier
A Piano Method, Ninth Exercise

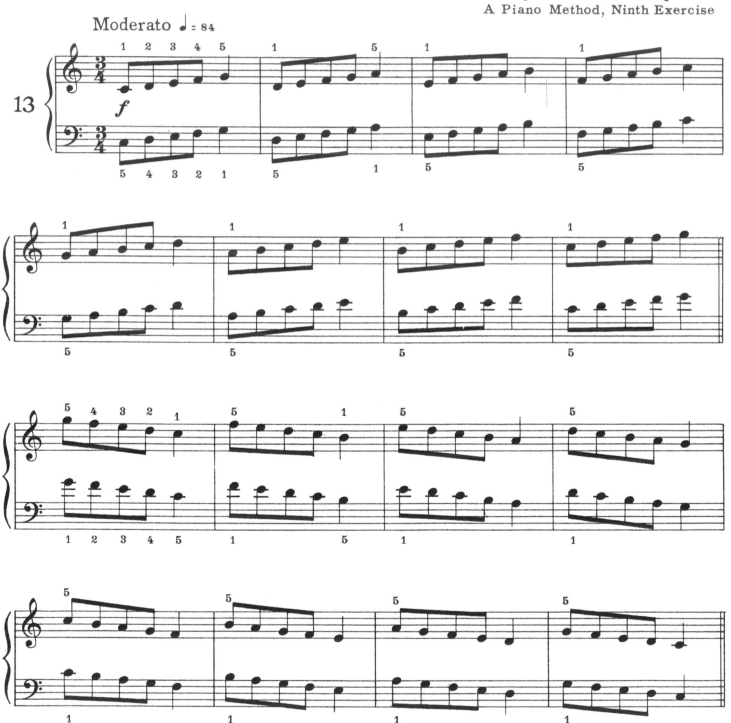

Study in the G position

Louis Köhler
Op. 218, No. 20

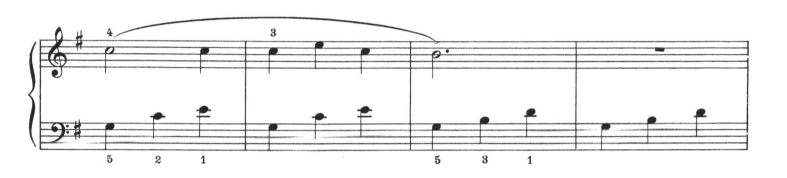

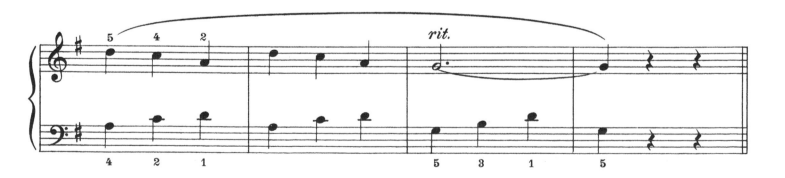

Study No. 15, like study No. 13, is also a five finger exercise. Unlike study No. 13 in which the fingers were played in consecutive order $\left(\overset{R.H.}{\overbrace{1\ 2\ 3\ 4}}\ 5,\ \overset{L.H.}{\overbrace{5\ 4\ 3\ 2}}\ 1\right)$, study No. 15 requires that the fingers be played in an alternating order: $1\ \overbrace{3\ 2\ 4\ 3}\ 5$ in the right hand and $\overbrace{5\ 3\ 4\ 2}\ 3\ 1$ in the left hand as the notes of the musical pattern ascend. The fingering of each hand is reversed as the notes of the musical pattern descend. Increased practicing is required to develop this more difficult study to a speed of ♩ = 96.

Adolphe-Clair Le Carpentier
A Piano Method, Tenth Exercise

Five finger exercise in
extended positions

Charles-Louis Hanon
The Virtuoso Pianist, No. 1

Original meter:

44959

Contrasting touches, *legato* and *staccato,* are developed in study No. 17. The opening chord should be played with a crisp *staccato.* It is immediately followed by a passage in the five finger position which must be played with a smooth *legato.* This alternating pattern of *staccato* and *legato* continues throughout the study and must be carefully observed.

Ludvig Schytte
Op. 108, No. 1

Study No. 18 will show how to develop a singing melodic line in one hand and a quiet accompaniment in the other. The melodic line is in the left hand in the first and third eight-measure sections (measures 1-8 and 17-24). In the middle section (measures 9-16) the melodic line is in the right hand.

It is necessary to apply more pressure *through* the hand that plays the melody than the hand that plays the accompaniment. The accompaniment must *always* be played more softly than the melody.

Cornelius Gurlitt
Op. 82, No. 60

Contrasting touch study

Ludvig Schytte
Op.108, No.13

Allegro moderato ♩ = 100

Study No. 20 is an exercise for the development of hand (or wrist) *staccato*. This *staccato* touch is developed in the following manner:

Place the hands upon the keys so that the hand, wrist and forearm form a level line.

Raise the hands above the keys, the motion occurring at the wrists *only*.

Drop the hands into the keys and return them immediately to their previously raised positions. The tones produced must be *staccato*.

Jean-Louis Streabbog
Op. 63, No. 3

Velocity study for the right hand

Louis Köhler
Op. 190, No. 31

Allegro ♩ = 116

*Original

44959

No. 22 is a study in expression. The important feature of this march is its strong rhythm, and the accents, indicated in the first measure, must be applied to the first and fourth counts of each measure throughout the piece. The chords mark *sf* (*sforzando*) in measures 8, 16 and 24 are played with a sudden, explosive emphasis. The left hand part contains the melody in measures 9 through 16. Careful attention to the pedal markings is required.

March of the Tin Soldiers

Cornelius Gurlitt
Op. 130, No. 6

Tempo di Marcia ♩. = 84

Velocity study for both hands

Cornelius Gurlitt
Op. 50, No. 2

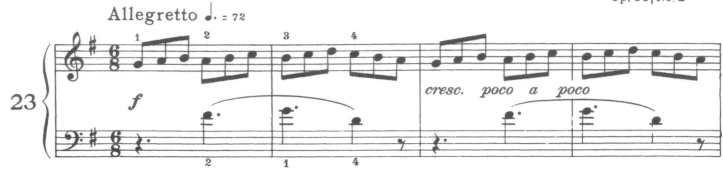

44959

Five finger exercise in
extended positions

Adolphe-Clair Le Carpentier
A Piano Method, Eleventh Exercise

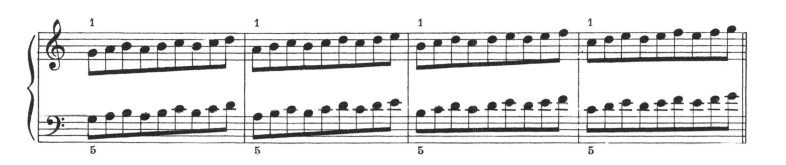

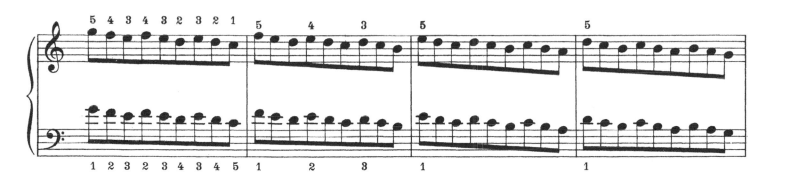

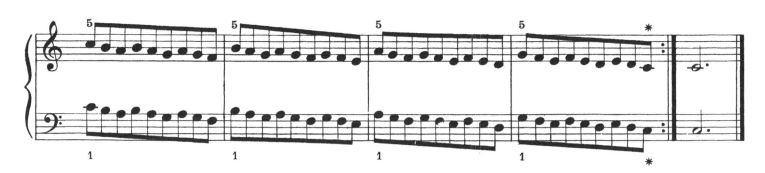

* added note

Study No. 25 will show you how to develop the technic of interlaced passage playing. In music passages of this sort the melodic figure passes constantly from one hand to the other. The dynamic level between the two hands must be precisely equal (in this instance, *p*). Each hand should be lifted from the keyboard as the succeeding hand enters. This will result in tonal purity and prevent any tonal muddiness caused by a dragging hand.

Cornelius Gurlitt
Op. 82, No. 44

Study for the development of
interlaced passage playing

Carl Czerny
Op. 261, No.53

Allegro ♩= 72

Study for the development of
interlaced passage playing
Pedal study

Louis Köhler
Op. 190, No. 33

Allegretto ♩ = 84

27

mf

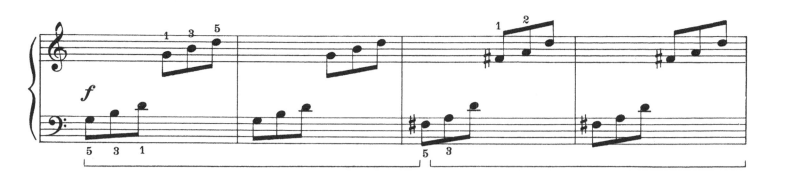

Study for the development of interlaced passage playing

Ludvig Schytte
Op.108, No.3

Study No. 29 is a phrasing study. The right hand part consists of a series of two - note phrases. Each of the tones of the two-note phrase is treated differently. The wrist is *lowered* as the first tone is played, thereby supplying an accent. The wrist is *raised* as the second tone is played, producing a tone that is much softer than the accented tone immediately preceding it. This alternation of heavy and light tones continues throughout this study.

The technic of this wrist action must be practiced at first with exaggerated motion. As the tempo is increased the wrist action becomes lesser.

Heinrich Wohlfahrt

*Original meter:

Velocity study for the left hand

Ludvig Schytte
Op. 108, No. 22

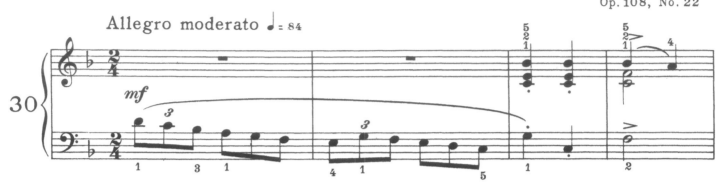

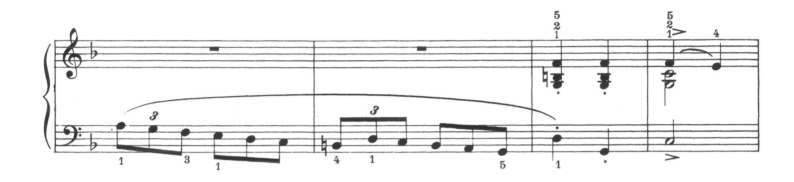

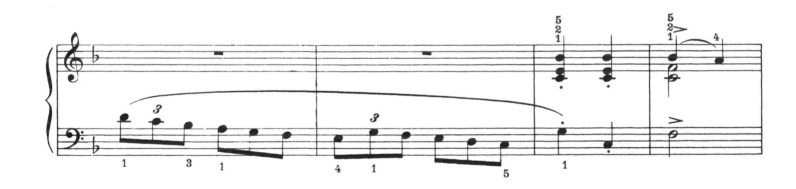

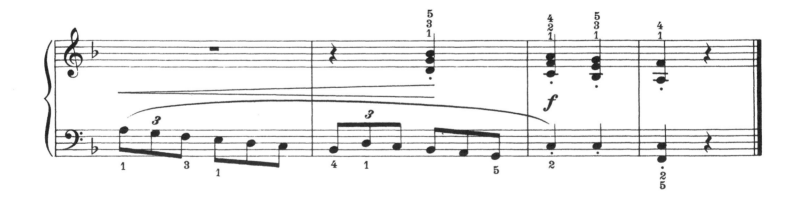

Rhythm study

Cornelius Gurlitt
Op. 82, No. 42

Velocity study for the right hand

Carl Czerny
Op. 261, No. 1

Velocity study for the left hand

Carl Czerny
Op. 261, No. 2

Velocity study for the right hand

Allegro ♩ = 92

Carl Czerny
Op. 261, No.5

34

Velocity study for the left hand

Allegro ♩ = 92

Carl Czerny
Op. 261, No.6

35

Velocity study for the right hand

Carl Czerny
Op. 261, No. 9

Allegro moderato ♩. = 60

Velocity study for the left hand

Carl Czerny
Op. 261, No. 10

Allegro moderato ♩. = 60

Velocity study for the right hand

Ludvig Schytte
Op. 108, No. 23

Allegro ♩. = 48

Study No. 39 is a scale study for both hands. The development of the technic of smooth scale performance is one of the major technical problems in piano playing. Two kinds of evenness are required: the equal spacing of all tones for *rhythmic evenness,* and the identical dynamic level of all tones for *tonal evenness.*

The hand must remain sti!l (with a minimum motion of the wrist) as the thumb passes under the fingers or the fingers pass over the thumb.

Conrad Kühner

Study in contrasting touches

Ludvig Schytte
Op. 108, No. 7

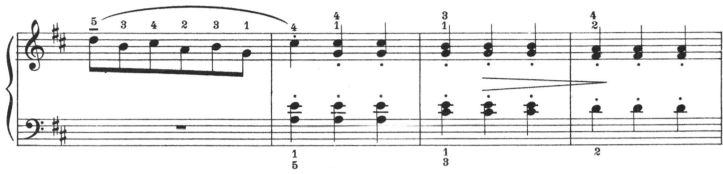

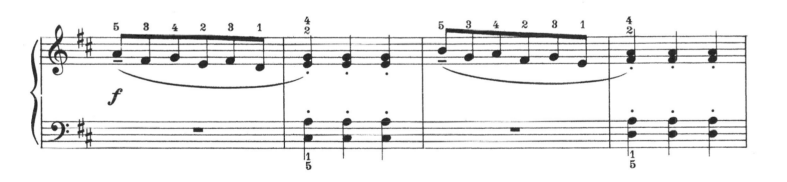

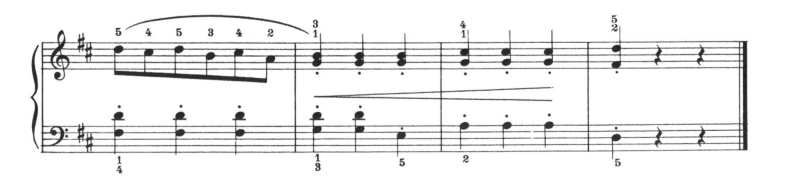

Scale study for both hands

Louis Streabbog
Op. 63, No.1

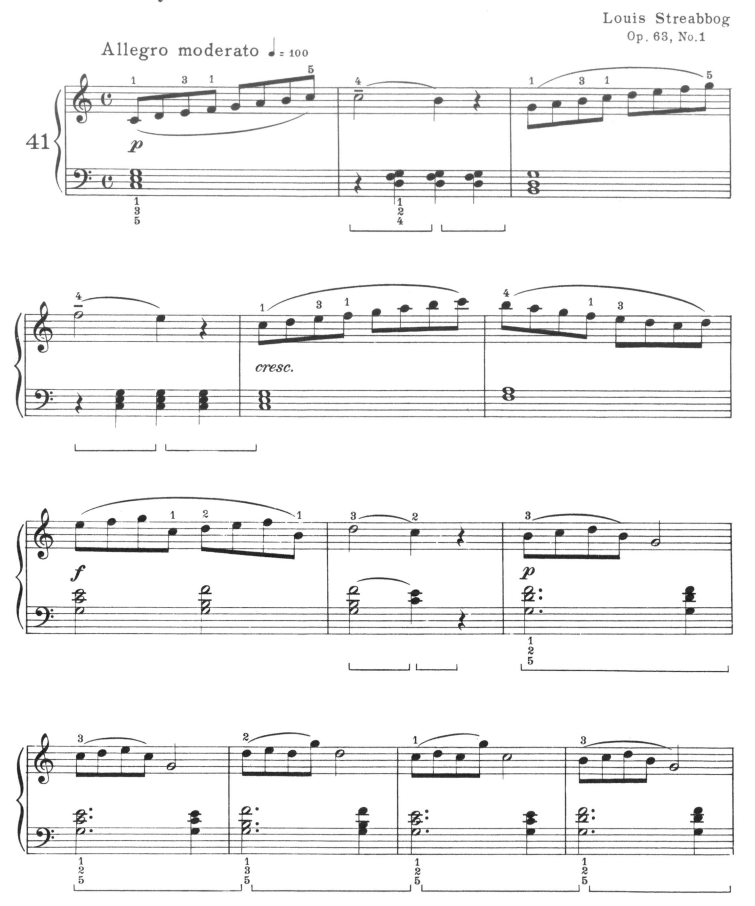

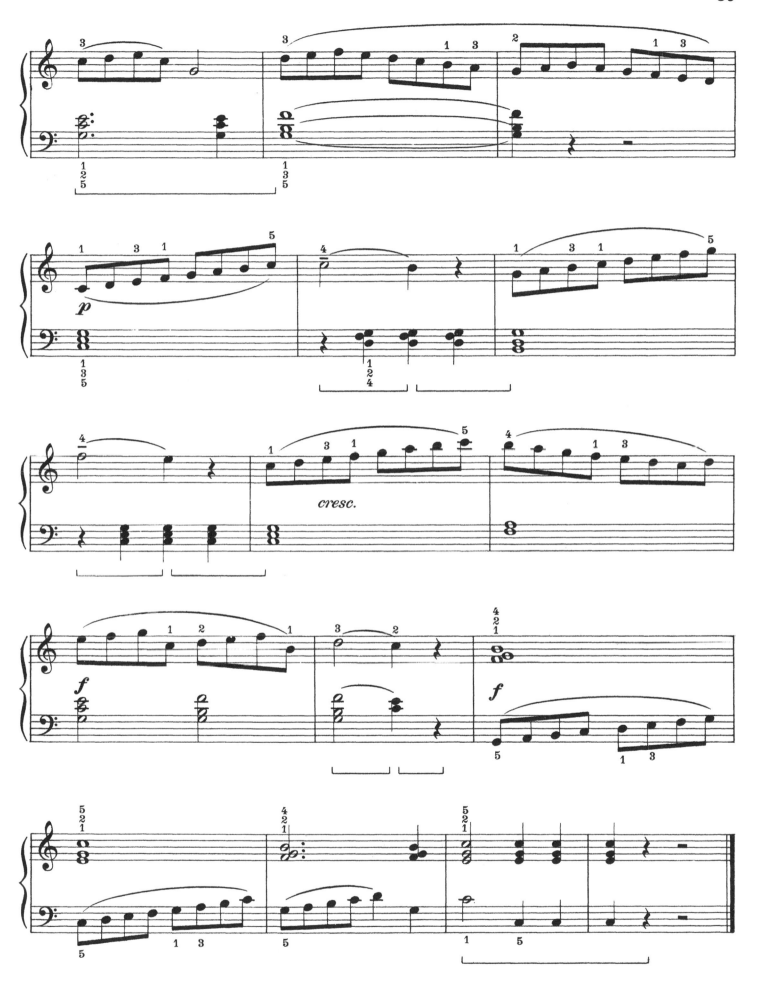

Study No. 42 is a study in the crossing of the left hand over the right hand. This motion of the left hand must be relaxed, graceful and unhurried. This motion should start soon after the left hand has played its lower (bass) tone, in order to remain unhurried as it approaches its upper (treble) tone.

The upper tone of the left hand should receive an accent. This, combined with careful pedalling, will produce a tone of bell-like quality.

Louis Streabbog
Op. 63, No. 6

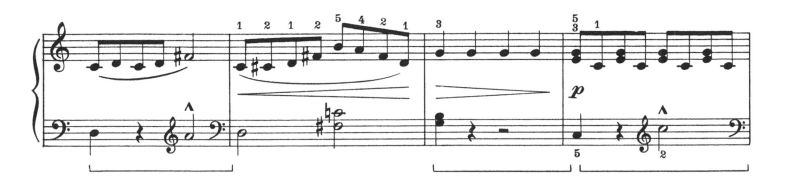

Velocity study for both hands

Félix Le Couppey
Op. 17, No. 6

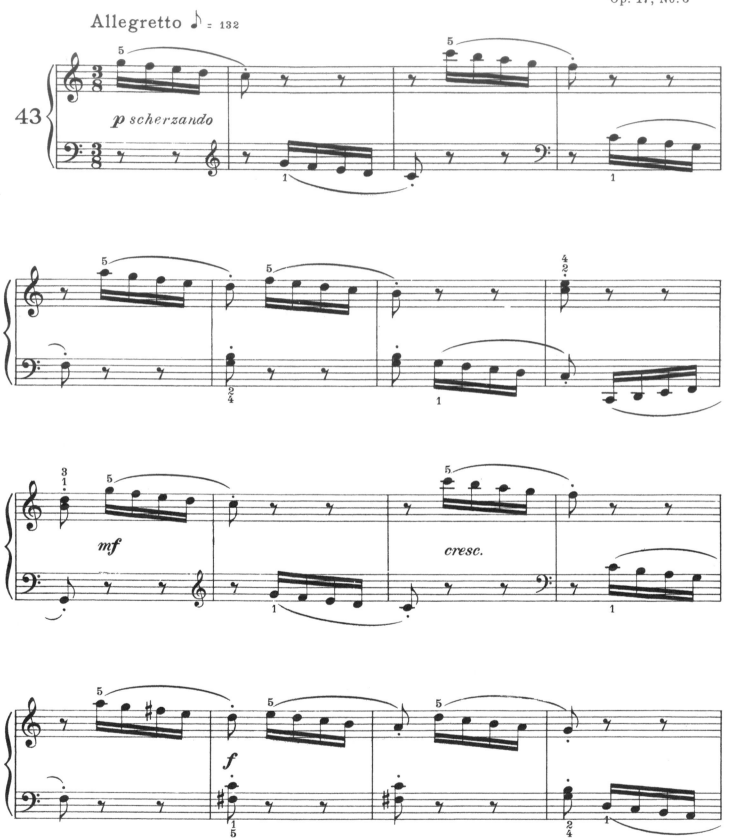

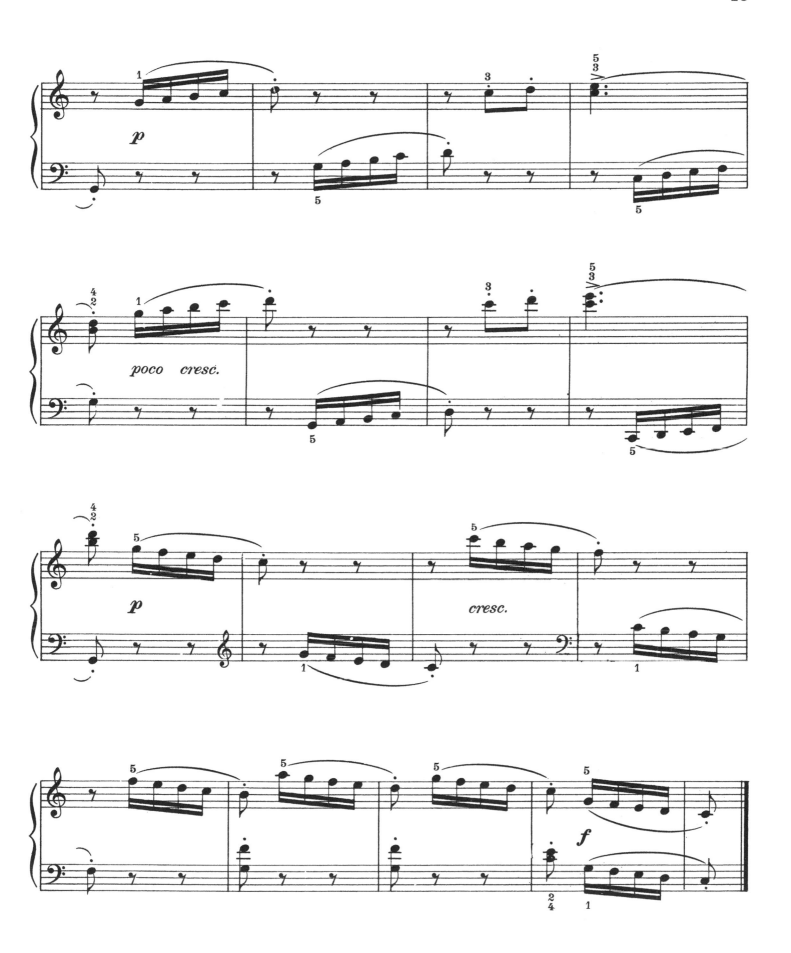

44959

Study in contrasting touches

Ludvig Schytte
Op. 108, No. 8

Study No. 45 introduces the technic of performing a rhythm indicated by a dotted eighth-note and a sixteenth-note. On the printed page, the sixteenth-note appears to be connected to the dotted eighth-note which precedes it (♪. ♪). However, the sixteenth-note is connected musically to the dotted eighth-note which *follows* it (♪. ♪.). The following preparatory study employs two methods of counting, both of which are to be practiced several times before playing this study:

45   Moderato ♩ = 80

Uso Seifert

Study in expression

Ludvig Schytte
Op. 108, No. 12

Study in contrasting touches
Study in rhythm

Cornelius Gurlitt
Op.82, No.34

Velocity study for both hands
Study in chords

Carl Czerny
First Instruction in
Piano Playing, No. 28

Study in interlaced passage playing

Joseph Concone
Op. 37, No. 2

Study in expression

Cornelius Gurlitt
Op. 130, No. 35

Adagio

Study in expression

Cornelius Gurlitt
Op. 130, No. 23

Scale study for both hands

Cornelius Gurlitt
Op. 82, No. 61

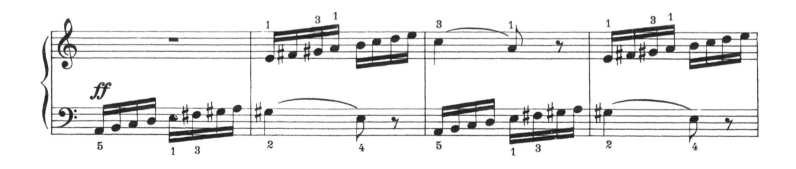

Study in chords

Ludvig Schytte
Op.108, No.25

Moderato deciso ♩ = 100

Scale study for the right hand

Gustav Damm
Method for the Pianoforte

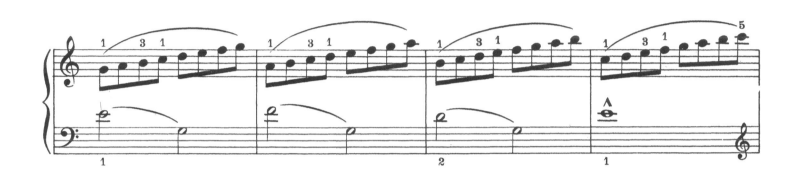

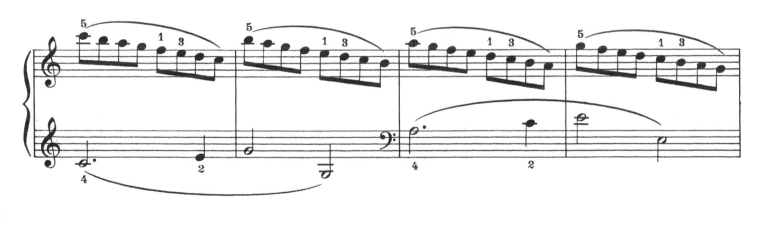

Scale study for the left hand

Gustav Damm
Method for the Pianoforte

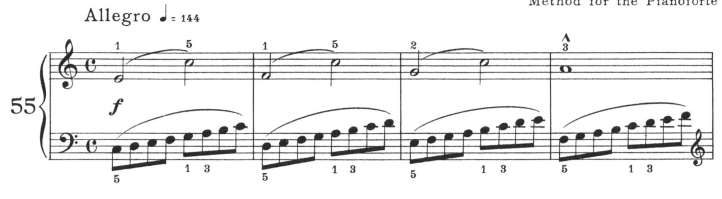

44959

Scale study for the right hand

Gustav Damm
Method for the Pianoforte

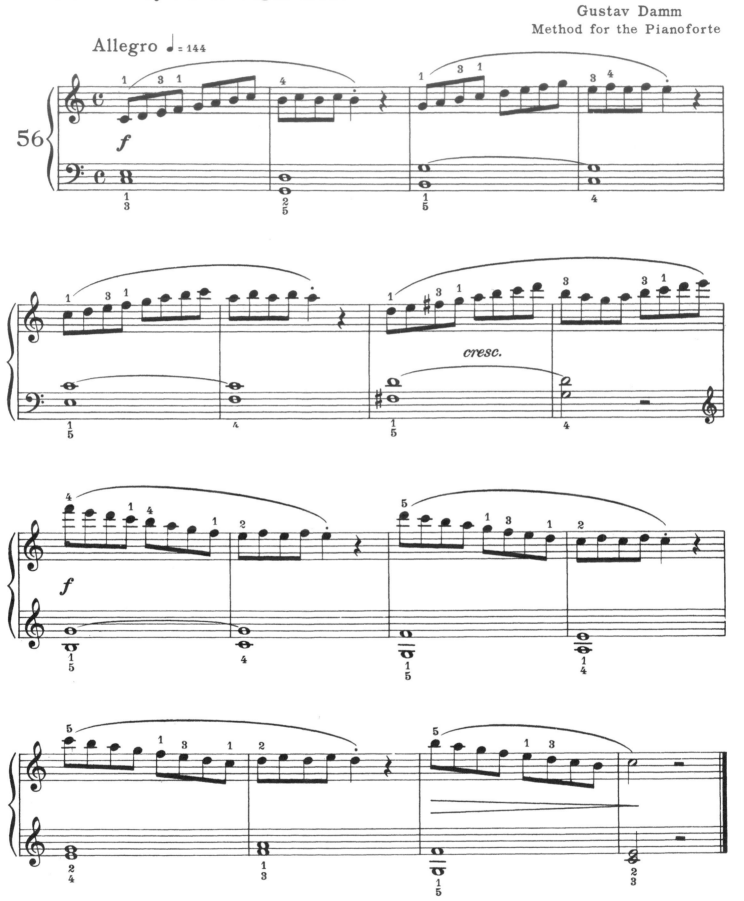

Scale study for the left hand

Gustav Damm
Method for the Pianoforte

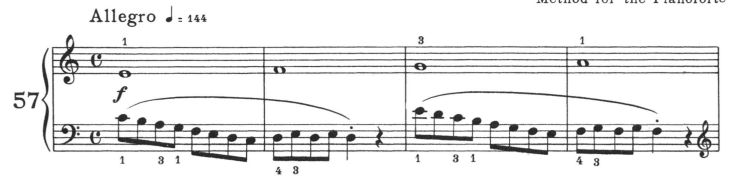

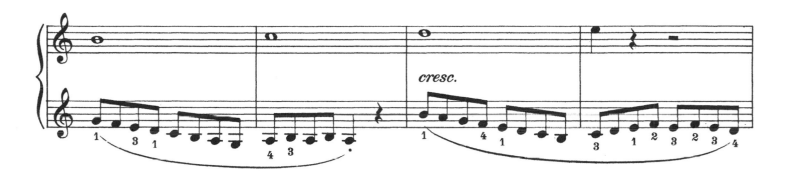

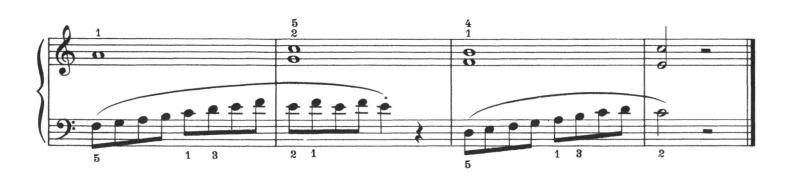

Velocity study for both hands

Edmund Parlow

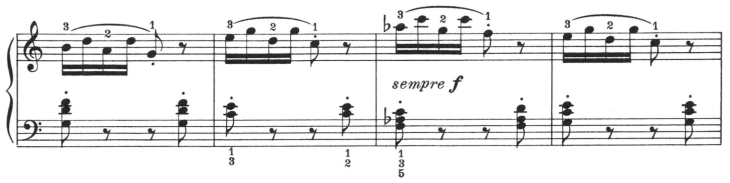

Study in expression
Chord study

Albert Biehl
Op. 44, No. 6

Velocity study for both hands

Cornelius Gurlitt
Op. 82, No. 59

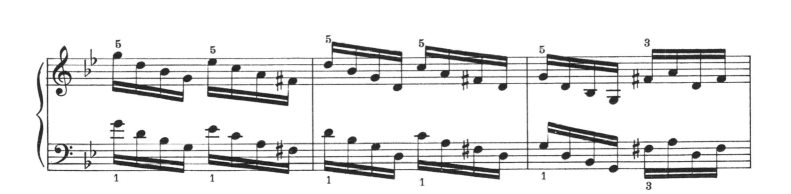

Study in expression

Anton Krause

Arabeske

Study in expression

Friedrich Burgmüller
Op. 100, No. 2